NELSON MANDELA

South Africa in the 1950s was a country rich in gold
and diamonds. With beautiful countryside, large
comfortable houses, and good weather, South Africans
had everything they needed for a wonderful life – if they
were white.

As a young lawyer, Nelson Mandela learned very quickly
about the difficult life of black South Africans – a life
with poor houses and schools, and where people could
not vote, or travel without a pass. And just as quickly he
decided that their struggle was his struggle too.

There were difficult years ahead – years of hiding from
the police, or separation from his family, of pain and
injustice. But those years made a man who could at last
be president of a new South Africa – a country where
people of all colours could have equal political rights.
This is the story of a man who was truly one of the great
leaders of our times, loved by millions across the world.

OXFORD BOOKWORMS LIBRARY
Factfiles

Nelson Mandela

Stage 4 (1400 headwords)

Factfiles Series Editor: Christine Lindop

ROWENA AKINYEMI

Nelson Mandela

OXFORD UNIVERSITY PRESS

OXFORD
UNIVERSITY PRESS

Great Clarendon Street, Oxford OX2 6DP

Oxford University Press is a department of the University of Oxford.
It furthers the University's objective of excellence in research, scholarship,
and education by publishing worldwide in

Oxford New York

Auckland Cape Town Dar es Salaam Hong Kong Karachi
Kuala Lumpur Madrid Melbourne Mexico City Nairobi
New Delhi Shanghai Taipei Toronto

With offices in

Argentina Austria Brazil Chile Czech Republic France Greece
Guatemala Hungary Italy Japan Poland Portugal Singapore
South Korea Switzerland Thailand Turkey Ukraine Vietnam

ISBN: 978 0 19 423396 5

A complete recording of this Bookworms edition of *Nelson Mandela* is available.

Printed in China

Word count (main text): 16,390

For more information on the Oxford Bookworms Library,
visit www.oup.com/elt/gradedreaders/

ACKNOWLEDGEMENTS

Illustration page 2 by Gareth Riddiford

The publishers would like to thank the following for permission to reproduce images:

AKG-images pp12 (Africa Media Online / Drum Social Histories / Baileys African History Archive),
19 (Africa Media Online), 44/45 (Africa Media Online); Alamy pp27 (Pictorial Press Ltd), 40
(robertharding); Baileys African History Archives p32; Camera Press pp18 (Ian Berry), 36 (Mark
Stewart), 56 (Jan Kopec), 72 (James Veysey); Getty Images pp11 (Popperfoto), 14 (Bettmann
Archive), 23 (Terence Spencer/The LIFE Images Collection), 39 (Louise Gubb/Corbis Historical),
42 (RooM RF), 47 (Mark Peters/Hulton Archive), 49 (Selwyn Tait/The LIFE Images Collection), 50
(Sahm Doherty/The LIFE Images Collection), 55 (Allan Tannenbaum/The LIFE Images Collection),
59 (William F. Campbell/The LIFE Images Collection), 6 (Terence Spencer/The LIFE Images
Collection), 62 (Walter Dhladhla/AFP), 68/69 (Frank Micelotta), 70/71 (Alexander Joe/AFP), 8
(Richard I'Anson/Lonely Planet Images), 9 (Hulton Archive); Press Association Images p64 (John
Stillwell/PA Archive); Reuters Media pp10 (Ulli Michel), 57 (Ulli Michel), 66 (Shannon Stapleton),
67 (Radu Sigheti); Rex Features - Shutterstock pp17 (Sipa Press), 4 (Sipa Press), cover (NILS
JORGENSEN); TopFoto p52 (Topham / AP); UWC - Robben Island Mayibuye Archives pp24/25, 3,
30, 34.

CONTENTS

The Transkei

1 The beginnings (1918–1941)

On 18 July 1918 a baby boy was born to the Mandela family in a small village just south of Qunu, in the Transkei province of South Africa. The child was given the name Rolihlahla, which means 'troublemaker' in the Xhosa language.

The Transkei is one of the most beautiful parts of South Africa, with hills and many rivers, beautiful flowers in the spring, and green trees all year round. Rolihlahla was one of thirteen children of a chief of the Thembu people. During his childhood he played games in the fields around Qunu with the other children of the village, looked after the sheep and cows, and swam in the cold river which came down from the hills.

At the age of seven, Rolihlahla went to school, the only one of his brothers and sisters to do so. And it was on his first day at school that his teacher, Miss Mdingane, gave him the English name of Nelson, the name which later became world-famous.

When he was nine, Nelson's father died and his mother took him to live with his uncle, Chief Jongintaba, the king of the Thembu people. Early one morning, Nelson and his mother left Qunu. It was a day's walk along rough roads to Nelson's new home. They did not talk as they walked, but much later Mandela wrote: 'The silence of the heart between mother and child is not a lonely one. My mother and I never talked very much, but we did not need to.' At last, when it was nearly dark, they reached the village of Mqhekezweni. Chief Jongintaba lived in a large home with gardens of apple trees, vegetables, and flowers. This was the Great Place of the Thembu, where Nelson lived with his uncle, aunt and cousins. Nelson saw how a leader should behave. He watched and listened while his uncle met his people in order to discuss the problems in their lives – the dry weather, or new laws made by the white government.

From his uncle, Nelson learned about the history of the

The Great Place of the Thembu

African people and the arrival of white people. The Thembu people are part of the Xhosa nation. The Xhosa are farming people who moved down from central Africa and have lived in the south-eastern areas of Ciskei and Transkei since the eleventh century.

The first white people arrived from Europe on the most southern coast of Africa in 1652. For the next 200 years the African nations who lived there (the Zulu, the Xhosa, the Sotho, and others) fought against the white people who took their land. But in the end, the old weapons of the African soldiers could not win against the modern guns of the soldiers from Europe.

Two groups of white people lived in South Africa: those from Britain who spoke English, and those from the Netherlands who became known as Afrikaners and spoke Afrikaans, a kind of Dutch. Although the British and the Afrikaners hated each other, these two groups learned to work together against the African people. In 1910, the Afrikaner Transvaal and Orange Free State joined the British Cape Province and Natal to become the four provinces of the Union of South Africa, a nation with a white government although about 70 per cent of the people who lived there were black.

The discovery of diamonds in the British city of Kimberley in 1867 and the discovery of gold in the Afrikaner province of Transvaal in 1886 had changed the history of South Africa. Africans were forced to dig in the diamond and gold mines, but the money from the gold and diamonds went to the white owners of the mines. African miners lived in poor conditions: about fifty men had to live in one room. Each

Nelson aged nineteen

black worker had to carry a pass – a paper signed by a white official – which showed that the worker was allowed to be near the mine.

In the 1920s, new laws prevented Africans from getting jobs with good pay and from owning land and houses in the towns. In the 1930s, white workers earned five times more than African workers.

In 1936, while Nelson was at school, the white parliament in Cape Town removed the right to vote from the few Africans who had it. A new law forced all African men to carry a pass in order to travel, to get a job, or to be out late at night. If an African was caught without a pass, he was put in prison. The government also decided that 87 per cent of the land in South Africa must be kept for the 2 million white people. Most of this land was the best land in the country.

The other 13 per cent of the land, most of it poor land, was left for the 8 million Africans.

In 1939, Chief Jongintaba sent Nelson to the University College of Fort Hare (the best college in South Africa for black students) about 100 kilometres away, near the small town of Alice. There were 150 African students at the College, and Nelson made friends with boys from other parts of South Africa, including a student called Oliver Tambo. Tambo was a year older than Nelson and they remained friends for life. At Fort Hare, Nelson enjoyed sport, playing football, and running, and he also spent hours in the evenings listening to music and dancing with other students.

At this time, Nelson's dream was to build his mother a new home in Qunu after he finished his studies. But his days at Fort Hare ended sooner than he had planned. At the end of his second year Nelson was elected to the students' committee, and he joined other students to protest about the food at the college, and to ask the teachers to listen to the opinions of the committee. The college told Nelson that unless he changed his mind about the protest, he could not return to the college for his final year.

During the holidays, Chief Jongintaba told Nelson that he must obey the college. The Chief also told Nelson that he had arranged marriages for Nelson and for his own son, Justice. It was the custom in those days for parents to arrange marriages for their children, but neither Justice nor Nelson wanted to marry the girls chosen for them. They were not strong enough to tell the Chief that they disagreed with him, so they decided to leave Mqhekezweni secretly and go north to Johannesburg, one of the biggest cities in South Africa, about 600 kilometres away.

2 Johannesburg (1941–1952)

In order to pay for their journey, the boys secretly sold two of the Chief's cows. African men had to carry a pass when they travelled, but although Nelson and Justice did not have the necessary papers, they travelled north first by train and then finally by car to Johannesburg. At about ten o'clock one evening they saw the lights of the city. 'I had reached the end of what seemed like a long journey,' Mandela wrote many years later, 'but it was actually the very beginning of a much longer and more trying journey.'

Johannesburg in the 1950s

Nelson began work as a guard at one of Johannesburg's gold mines, but the news of his escape from home followed him and he lost the job. A cousin then introduced him to Walter Sisulu, a businessman several years older than Nelson. Walter Sisulu had worked in many jobs – deep under the ground in a gold mine, in the kitchen of a white family, and in a factory – and used his time in the evenings to study. It was Walter who found Nelson a job in the office of a white lawyer called Lazar Sidelsky who was interested in African schools and who taught Nelson a lot about the law.

Johannesburg was the richest city in South Africa, with the largest gold mines in the world. The people of South Africa called it the 'city of gold'. In 1939, more than 320,000 Africans worked in the gold mines of Johannesburg. There were 43,000 white workers, who earned over eleven times more than the black workers. Between 1933 and 1966, 19,000 gold miners died in accidents there, and 93 per cent of them were Africans.

In Johannesburg, Nelson saw more cars and more tall buildings than he had ever seen before, but he also saw for the first time the injustice of life in South Africa. He lived in the African township of Alexandra, far from the large, beautiful houses where rich white people lived and enjoyed the wealth from the mines. The townships were the areas outside the city where black people had to live. There was no running water or electricity, and the houses were poor and crowded. Nelson was so poor that he often walked the 10 kilometres to work and then the 10 kilometres back again, and for five years he wore the same suit to work.

Another African worked in Sidelsky's office. Gaur Radebe was interested in political ideas, and at lunch times he talked to Nelson about the history of Africa and the living conditions of black Africans in South Africa. Nelson and Gaur joined 10,000 people marching through the streets of Alexandra. They were protesting about a rise in the price of travelling on the buses. The buses ran empty for nine days; then the bus company put the prices down again.

In 1941 Chief Jongintaba visited Johannesburg. Nelson was worried about seeing his uncle for the first time since he ran away from Mqhekezweni, but the Chief was kind to Nelson and talked only about his future, not his past. A few months later Chief Jongintaba died and Nelson and Justice travelled back home to Mqhekezweni. Justice stayed at the Great Place and became the new king of the Thembu people, but Nelson returned to Johannesburg. Although Nelson's heart was with his family and people, he knew that he wanted a different life for himself.

Nelson began to study law in the evenings at the University of Witwatersrand, where for the first time he studied with white students. It was here that he became friends with Joe Slovo, Ruth First, and Bram Fischer, whose father was president of one of the Afrikaner provinces of South Africa. Most of the white students, however, did not want to talk to or sit next to a black student.

Nelson often visited the house of Walter and Albertina Sisulu, for meals and long conversations about the rights and living conditions of black Africans in South Africa. It was there that Nelson met and fell in love with a pretty girl called Evelyn Mase who was training to be a nurse and who worked with Albertina. They soon married and moved into their own home, Number 8115 Orlando West (another African township which later became part of Soweto). In 1946 their son Thembekile was born, followed in 1947 by their first daughter. She was often ill, and for many nights

Nelson and Evelyn stayed awake taking care of her. When she was nine months old, their daughter died, which was a great sadness to them.

Nelson and Oliver Tambo (who was now living in Johannesburg) began to go to meetings of the African National Congress with Walter Sisulu. The African National Congress (ANC) was

Mandela in the 1940s

started in 1912 by four young African lawyers. They wanted to change South Africa so that Africans could be elected to parliament and could own land; they believed that Africans should work together to get better conditions for black people in South Africa.

Nelson soon became very involved in the work of the organization and by 1947, when he was elected to the ANC committee of the Transvaal province, he felt ready to give his heart fully to the work of the ANC.

The elections of 1948, in which only white people could vote, were won by the Afrikaner National Party, led by Dr Daniel Malan. The National Party did not want black people to enjoy the wealth of the country or have a part in the political life of South Africa. Dr Malan introduced a political system called 'apartheid': a new word, but an old idea. There were laws to separate white and black people in all areas of life: schools, work, hospitals, housing areas, and even marriage. From 1948, 'Whites Only' signs appeared in many places: taxis, ambulances, buses, restaurants, hotels, parks, and even beaches. In sports, too, white and black people could not play together.

Mandela finished his studies in 1952 and became a lawyer. With Oliver Tambo, he opened the first African law office in Johannesburg, in a small building near the centre of the city. Crowds came to the new office, because they knew that the African lawyers would give them good advice. Mandela and Tambo heard about land that was taken from Africans and given to white people. They heard about people who were kicked and beaten by the police. They were busy all day long, and then in the evenings they went to political meetings.

On 26 June 1952, after many months of careful planning, the Defiance Campaign began. The ANC, the Communist Party, and the Indian Congress all worked together on this campaign. Africans worked with Indians (brought to South Africa in the 1860s by the British government as cheap workers) and with Coloured people (whose parents had a

different skin colour from each other). The idea behind the campaign was to show defiance – to refuse to obey the laws that were not fair. All over South Africa non-white people used Whites Only entrances to railway stations and offices and entered townships without passes.

During the campaign, Mandela drove all over the country in order to explain the campaign to the Africans living in the townships. He worked so hard that his little son Thembekile asked his mother, 'Where does Daddy live?' The campaign continued for six months, and during that time the police arrested more than 8,000 people. Mandela and Walter Sisulu were arrested, with other members of the ANC. Among the Indians arrested was Ahmed Kathrada, a young man aged twenty-one, who soon became another good friend of Mandela's. They were kept in prison for two days and then released.

The campaign was a new experience for Mandela. He became more confident because the campaign showed white people that Africans were not afraid to fight against the system of apartheid and that they had not lost their dignity.

The Defiance Campaign

3 Working for the ANC (1953–1960)

Sophiatown was an African township only 6 kilometres west of the centre of Johannesburg. It was one of the few places where Africans had been able to buy houses and many had lived there for more than fifty years. Because Sophiatown was close to the centre of the city, several families lived in each home, with as many as forty people getting their water from a single tap.

Sophiatown was surrounded by towns where white workers lived, and the government wanted to move white workers

Sophiatown in the 1950s

into Sophiatown. In 1953, the government started to force Africans out of their homes in Sophiatown to a new township about 20 kilometres from the city. This was part of the government's plan to control where Africans could live and work.

The ANC organized meetings in Sophiatown for many months, as they tried to prevent the government's plan to destroy the township. Mandela spoke at these meetings until September 1953, when he was banned for two years under a law introduced in 1950. This law allowed the government to stop any person from going to meetings, leaving town, belonging to political organizations, or meeting friends. Although Mandela was not accused of any crime, for two years he was forbidden to go to any meetings or to leave Johannesburg, and he was even unable to go to his son's birthday party. He was also forced to leave the ANC. (Most of the ANC leaders were banned for many years.)

Mandela was unable to go to the national meeting of the ANC in September 1953, and another member of the ANC read his words for him. Mandela said that Africans must be prepared for a different type of struggle. He believed that truth would win, and that injustice would be defeated. But he told them: 'There is no easy walk to freedom. Many of us will have to pass through the valley of the shadow of death again and again before we reach the mountain tops of our desires.' These words became famous. Mandela had read about the difficulties and bravery of the Indian leader Pandit Nehru (1889–1964), and he took the words 'No easy walk to freedom' from Nehru.

At the beginning of 1955, 4,000 police and soldiers arrived at Sophiatown and began to move people out and to destroy their homes. The ANC had failed to save Sophiatown and

Mandela began to realize that the government would not listen to the ANC's non-violent protests.

In 1953, the government had passed a law which separated the African school system from the white school system in order to force African children to go to poorer schools. Dr

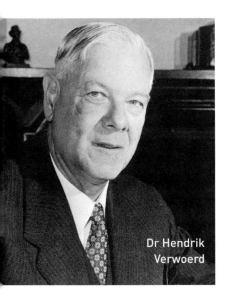

Dr Hendrik
Verwoerd

Hendrik Verwoerd, who was minister of African schools at that time, said that the only place for Africans in South Africa was in some types of work. He meant that Africans would only do boring, badly paid work, so they did not need to go to expensive schools. The ANC organized protests about this law and Mandela wanted Africans to set up their own schools. In the 1950s, the government spent 44 pounds every year for

each white student, 19 pounds for each Coloured and Asian student, and less than 8 pounds for each African student. (After 1959, all universities were forbidden to accept black students without the agreement of the government, and by 1978, 80 per cent of university students were white.)

In June 1955 a Congress of the People was organized by the ANC and many other groups which were working for freedom. The Congress was organized to discuss the Freedom Charter, which was a list of ideas from all the groups. It was held in Kliptown, a village a few kilometres outside Johannesburg, and Mandela and Walter Sisulu had to drive there secretly because they were both banned. For two days about 3,000 people discussed the Freedom Charter. The Freedom Charter became important in the struggle for freedom because it described the wishes of Africans for a free South Africa. It said that every man and woman should be able to vote for the government, that all national groups should have equal rights, and that the land and wealth of the nation should be shared by all people.

Most of the people at the Congress were black but there were also Indian and Coloured people and more than one hundred white people. On the afternoon of the second day, police with guns surrounded the meeting and wrote down the name of every person there. But Mandela had seen the police arrive and quickly returned to Johannesburg.

In September 1955, Mandela's ban ended and he was free to travel. He had been looking forward to leaving the city and returning to the hills of his childhood. He visited Qunu and Mqhekezweni for the first time for thirteen years. He was happy to see his mother, sister, and old friends, to walk in the fields where he had played as a child, and to look up at the stars at night. He asked his mother to come and live with him in Johannesburg, but she did not want to leave the countryside. Mandela then travelled to Cape Town, Port Elizabeth, and other parts of South Africa in order to meet members of the ANC, before driving back to Johannesburg, along the beautiful beaches of the Indian Ocean.

Early one morning in December 1956, Mandela was woken by loud knocks on the door of his home in Orlando West. It was the police, who searched the house for more than an hour before arresting Mandela and taking him to Johannesburg's old prison, the Fort. There Mandela discovered that the police had arrested 156 people: members of the ANC and other freedom groups who had been at

Kliptown. They were all forced to take off their clothes and stand for an hour in the cold air, before being taken to two large cells where they were kept for two weeks.

At last they were taken to court and charged with treason. The government said that the ideas of the Freedom Charter were communist. This proved, the government said, that the freedom groups were planning to destroy the government. The 156 accused were allowed to leave prison but they had to report to the police once a week and were forbidden to go to any meetings while they waited for the trial to begin.

When Mandela returned home, he discovered that Evelyn had moved out with the children and gone to live with her brother. The marriage was over. Mandela's work with the ANC had given him little time with his family. Evelyn had become more and more involved with her church, and slowly they had begun to live separate lives. All of their children were hurt by this, and Mandela continued to visit them often. He was still their father, although he was no longer Evelyn's husband.

Bram Fischer and the other lawyers prepared for the trial for many months. During this time Mandela met a lovely young woman in Oliver Tambo's office, and he knew at once that he wanted to marry her. Winnie Madikizela had just finished training and was working at an African hospital in Johannesburg. They were married in 1958. In the difficult times that lay ahead, Winnie's love would help to make Mandela strong.

The treason trial began in August 1958. In the end, thirty of the accused went to court. Every day, Mandela, Walter Sisulu, Ahmed Kathrada, and the others went by bus with their lawyers to the court in Pretoria, a two-hour journey away. At lunchtimes they sat outside in a friend's garden and

Mandela and Winnie, 1958

ate lunch which was cooked by their Indian friends. In the evenings Mandela went back to Johannesburg to catch up with all his work at the law office and to go to ANC meetings.

In 1958, while the treason trial continued, Dr Hendrik Verwoerd became Prime Minister. He wanted Africans to be separated from white people even more than before, so one of the first things he said as Prime Minister was that all Africans must be called 'Bantus'. In 1959 he created eight Bantustans, where black people had to live with their chiefs. Black people could no longer expect any rights in the parts of South Africa which white people controlled.

The treason trial was stopped suddenly on 21 March 1960. On that morning, there was a terrible disaster at Sharpeville, a small township about 55 kilometres south of Johannesburg. The Pan-Africanist Congress (PAC), a new African organization, had organized a protest against the pass laws. As part of this protest, a crowd of several thousand marched to the police station in Sharpeville without their passes. The crowd waited quietly, but as the crowd got larger the police became more worried. Suddenly the police began to shoot at the crowd. People turned and tried to run away, but the

The Sharpeville shooting

police continued to shoot. When they stopped shooting, sixty-nine people had been killed.

Protests against the deaths came from all over the world, including the United Nations (in fact, this was the first time that the United Nations spoke out about what was happening in South Africa). Thousands of Africans, including Chief Luthuli, Mandela, and other members of the ANC, burned their passes to protest against the apartheid government's terrible crime, and the police arrested 18,000 people.

In these difficult times the ANC decided that Oliver Tambo must leave South Africa in order to organize the ANC abroad. The Mandela and Tambo law office was shut, and Tambo escaped from South Africa. The police knocked again at Mandela's door and his house was searched again. Mandela was taken to Pretoria Prison, with the other thirty accused, where they were kept in small, dirty cells, and the treason trial continued.

In August 1960, Mandela finally spoke at the trial, and he was questioned about many of his ideas. Mandela told the court that the ANC wanted all people of South Africa to be able to vote for their government. They were prepared to organize protests until the government said, "Let's talk". Then they would agree to talk.

In March 1961, more than four years after the first arrests, the trial ended. 'You are found not guilty,' the judge said. 'You may go.' Outside the court the crowd danced and sang the national song of the ANC, *Nkosi Sikelel' iAfrika*. The name of the song means 'God bless Africa', asking God to protect the African people, and it was composed in 1897 by Enoch Sontonga, a teacher in Johannesburg. It was written in Xhosa, and was sung as a protest song during the years of apartheid. Now it is famous all over the world as the national song of South Africa, and it is sung in many languages of the South African people, including Afrikaans.

Mandela did not go home that night. After many meetings, the ANC leaders had decided to continue working secretly. Mandela was asked to travel secretly around the country and organize protests. Mandela's eldest son, Thembekile, was away at school, but he went to say goodbye to his two children who were living in Orlando East with their mother Evelyn. Then he went home and said goodbye to his two youngest daughters, Zenani (Zeni) and Zindziswa (Zindzi). 'I will be going away for a long time,' he told their mother Winnie. His new life 'underground' had begun.

The treason trial

The Spear of the Nation (1961–1962)

4

Mandela continued his work for the ANC. He knew he could be sent to prison if the police found out about his work. Mandela moved secretly from place to place for some months. He wore glasses and a dirty blue uniform with a driver's hat as he drove to meetings in the townships and in the villages. He began organizing African workers to hold a stay-at-home – a protest in which workers refuse to go to work – in order to force the government to organize a national meeting for all South Africans. Several times the police nearly caught him. Once he stopped at some traffic lights and saw a chief policeman sitting in the car next to him. Another afternoon in Johannesburg, an African policeman walked towards him. As he passed, the policeman smiled at Mandela and secretly gave him the thumbs-up ANC sign.

For a few weeks, Mandela stayed with Wolfie Kodesh, a newspaper man, in his small flat in a white part of the city. He stayed inside the flat during the day, and went out to meetings at night. Every morning he woke up early and ran in the small sitting room for an hour, to keep himself healthy. It is a custom of the Xhosa people to drink thick milk, and Mandela kept a bottle of this milk outside the window of the flat. One day, as he sat in the sitting room, Mandela heard two Africans talking as they walked past the flat. It was strange, they said, to see a bottle of Xhosa milk outside a white man's flat – and at that moment Mandela knew he had to leave Wolfie's flat.

The police made many arrests at this time, in order to prevent the stay-at-home. On 29 May 1961, thousands of Africans (joined by Indian and Coloured workers) stayed home from work, in Durban, Cape Town, Port Elizabeth, and Johannesburg. But the stay-at-home was not a success in all parts of the country and the government did not listen to the call for a national meeting.

In 1961, B. J. Vorster became Minister of Justice. He told the police they could forget about the rights of Africans. After the treason trial, the government realized that the courts and judges were not going to do everything the government wanted, and so the police were now given the freedom to beat and torture anyone they arrested.

On Freedom Day in June 1961, Mandela sent a letter to all the newspapers. He again asked the government to call a national meeting to talk about the freedom Africans wanted. He promised that he would continue to fight against apartheid. 'I will not leave South Africa. The struggle is my life. I will continue fighting for freedom until the end of my days.'

But the government refused to listen and Mandela now believed that violence was necessary in order to change the government's ideas. After discussing this with Walter Sisulu, Mandela went to a secret meeting of ANC leaders in Durban. The meeting continued all night. For fifty years the ANC had been non-violent, but at the end of this meeting, Mandela was asked to organize a new group. This new group was separate from the ANC and was called *Umkhonto we Sizwe* (the Spear of the Nation), or MK. MK was going to use violence to fight against the government. The fighting weapon in the group's name – the spear – showed that a different kind of struggle was beginning.

Mandela asked Joe Slovo to join this new group. Joe Slovo, an old friend, was a member of the Communist Party, which had already decided that violence was necessary in order to change South Africa.

In October, Mandela moved to Lilliesleaf Farm in Rivonia, a few kilometres north of Johannesburg, and he arranged some false papers: he became David Motsamayi, and worked as cook and driver to the white members of MK. Winnie visited Mandela for weekends, with their two daughters, Zeni and Zindzi. At Lilliesleaf, the members of MK lived together and planned the work of the new group. They decided that MK would destroy power stations and railways, in order to make things difficult for the government. Members of MK were told that they must not kill or injure people.

On 10 December 1961, Chief Luthuli received the Nobel Peace Prize for his work as leader of the ANC and for the ANC's long history of non-violence. Chief Luthuli (1898–1967) was the first African to receive the Nobel Peace Prize. The government gave him special permission to go to Norway to receive the prize. A week later, on 16 December 1961, the first MK bombs exploded at power stations and government offices in Johannesburg, Port Elizabeth, and Durban. The time of non-violence was over.

In January 1962, Mandela escaped from South Africa to go to a meeting of African leaders in Addis Ababa, Ethiopia. He drove secretly out of South Africa into Bechuanaland (now Botswana) and then flew to Dar es Salaam, where he met Julius Nyerere, the first President of Tanganyika. Then he went on to Addis Ababa, where he met Emperor Haile Selassie, and for the first time he saw African soldiers

Chief Luthuli

commanded by an African leader. He also met Kenneth Kaunda, who later became the President of Zambia. At this meeting of African leaders, Mandela thanked the African countries that were helping the fight against apartheid.

Oliver Tambo, who was living and working for the ANC in Dar es Salaam, travelled with Mandela to various African countries. They arranged training for MK members and they met freedom fighters from other African countries. Mandela also met his old friend Gaur Radebe, who was now a member of the PAC. In Dar es Salaam, on his way back to South Africa, Mandela met the first group of MK members who were travelling to Ethiopia to train as soldiers. Mandela felt proud to meet these brave young men. Everywhere Mandela went in Africa, he found that it was his character that mattered, not the colour of his skin. For the first time he felt free from the injustice of apartheid.

At last, Mandela flew back to Botswana, and he drove all night back into South Africa with Cecil Williams, a white member of MK. Once again, he became David Motsamayi. They returned to Lilliesleaf Farm in Rivonia, and after discussing his visits to other African countries with the members of MK, Mandela and Cecil left Lilliesleaf for secret meetings with the ANC in Durban.

When these meetings were finished, Mandela and Cecil began the 700-kilometre drive back to Johannesburg. Mandela was wearing his driver's coat, and they talked

Oliver Tambo and Mandela in Addis Ababa

about their political plans as they left the waters of the Indian Ocean behind them and drove through the beautiful green hills of Natal. They had only driven about a hundred kilometres when Mandela noticed a car filled with white men slowing down in front of the car he was driving. When he looked behind, he saw two more cars filled with white men. Mandela knew immediately that his life 'underground' was over. If he tried to jump from the car and escape into the trees, the police would kill him at once. So he pushed his gun and papers down the side of the car seat, where the police never found them. It was August 1962.

After his arrest, Mandela was taken to the Fort in Johannesburg and locked in a cell alone. Winnie was allowed to visit him in prison. They talked about which friends

would help Winnie, and how she would manage alone. Mandela asked her to tell the children the truth about his arrest.

Crowds of people protested against Mandela's arrest and when the trial began in Pretoria, crowds waited outside the court. Winnie was in court, wearing colourful Xhosa clothes. When Mandela entered the court, also wearing Xhosa clothes, the crowd stood up and there were shouts of *'Amandla! Ngawethu!'* (Power! To the people!)

Mandela was accused of organizing a stay-at-home by African workers. He was also charged with leaving South Africa without travel papers. Mandela told the court of his feelings about apartheid. 'I hate apartheid. I have fought it all my life. I fight it now and I will do so until the end of my days.' He said that he was not guilty of any crime, and when he came out of prison, he would take up the struggle against injustice again.

The day before Mandela was sentenced, the United Nations asked all countries to refuse to buy anything from South Africa.

In November 1962, Mandela was sentenced to five years in prison. Mandela turned to the crowd in the court. *'Amandla!'* he shouted three times. The people began to sing the beautiful ANC song *Nkosi Sikelel' iAfrika* and Mandela still heard them singing as the police drove him away.

For six months Mandela was kept in Pretoria prison. Now that he was a prisoner, not someone waiting for trial, he had to wear the prison uniform of African prisoners, which was short trousers and a shirt. The food was cold porridge, twice a day. For many hours every day the prisoners sat outside on the ground and sewed bags for the post office. While he worked, Mandela was able to talk occasionally to other

Mandela doing prison work

political prisoners, for example Robert Sobukwe, the leader
of the PAC. Sobukwe was in prison for three years, but as
soon as he was released he was re-arrested. Unlike Mandela,
Sobukwe refused to protest about prison conditions. (The
PAC disagreed with the Freedom Charter, and did not allow
white people, Indians, or communists into their group.)

One night at the end of May, Mandela was told to pack
his things. He was driven all night in a police truck without
windows with three other political prisoners to Cape Town
(about 1,500 kilometres away). The prisoners were then
taken in an old wooden boat to Robben Island.

Robben Island is a small, flat island about 11 kilometres
off the coast of Cape Town. In 1819 a famous Xhosa leader,
Makana, was put in prison there by the British government,
but he drowned as he tried to escape from the island. The
island was used as a prison by the apartheid government and
became known all over the world because of its famous
prisoners.

When Mandela and the other prisoners arrived on the
island, the guards marched them from the boat to the prison.
They were forced to take off their clothes, and the guards
threw the clothes onto the floor which was covered with
water. Then the guards told them to put their cold, wet
clothes back on.

Mandela knew that life on Robben Island was going to be
difficult, but he was only there for a few weeks before he was
taken back to Pretoria. On 11 July the police had surrounded
Lliesleaf Farm and arrested Walter Sisulu and eight other
members of MK. Mandela was back in court – this time
accused of sabotage.

5 The Rivonia trial (1963–1964)

In July 1963, the Rivonia trial began. In 1962, a new law had given the courts the power to give death sentences for crimes of sabotage, and anyone who owned a weapon could be charged with sabotage. In court with Mandela and Walter Sisulu were Govan Mbeki, Ahmed Kathrada, and Lionel Bernstein (all three were members of the Communist Party as well as members of the ANC), Raymond Mhlaba (a leader of the ANC and MK in the Cape Province), Elias Motsoaledi and Andrew Mlangeni (both members of the ANC), and Dennis Goldberg, who was the youngest of the accused.

During the 1960s, the police began using torture while questioning prisoners. In 1963, Looksmart Solwandle Ngudle, a member of the ANC, was the first political prisoner to die while police were questioning him.

Bram Fischer was one of the members of MK who was not at Lilliesleaf when the police surrounded the farm. He avoided arrest and so he was able to lead the team of lawyers. Every day the accused met their lawyers in order to prepare for the trial. Bram told his friends that they were charged with sabotage and that the government lawyers were going to ask for the death sentence.

As a prisoner, Mandela at first had to appear in court wearing his prison uniform. (Later, he was allowed to wear a suit.) At first Winnie was not allowed to go to the trial, but later she was allowed to go but forbidden to wear Xhosa

Bram Fischer

clothes in court. Both Albertina Sisulu and Caroline Motsoaledi were unable to go to the trial of their husbands because they were in prison, arrested under the Ninety-Day Detention Law. This law allowed the police to arrest any person suspected of a political crime and keep them in prison for up to ninety days without charging them with any crime or letting them see a lawyer.

Hundreds of papers had been found by the police at Lilliesleaf Farm, as well as maps which showed power stations and railways, but they found no weapons. The most important person to speak against the accused at the trial was Bruno Mtolo. Mtolo had been a member of the ANC and a member of MK, but now he was helping the police. Mandela and the others found it difficult to believe that someone they had worked with was helping to send them to prison and possibly to death.

From the beginning, the accused decided to accept the charge of sabotage. They wanted to use the trial to explain their ideas and to continue their struggle against apartheid. Much later, Kathrada remembered, 'Right through the trial, right from day one, he led us, he guided us. From the first day, he said, "This is a political trial."'

Mandela was the first to speak in court. He told the court that he was one of the people who had organized *Umkhonto we Sizwe*. He explained to the court that, although he was not a communist himself, the Communist Party was the only political group in South Africa which believed in the equality of Africans. Mandela spoke about the difference between the lives of black people and the lives of white people in South Africa. Because of apartheid, Africans experienced no dignity in their lives, but Africans wanted a fair share in the whole of South Africa. 'Above all, we want equal political rights,' he said. 'This . . . is what the ANC is fighting for. It is a struggle of the African people.'

Mandela spoke for over four hours. Then he put down his papers and turned to the judge, Justice de Wet. During his lifetime, he said, he had given himself to this struggle of the African people. He believed in a nation where all people lived together with equal rights. If necessary, he was prepared to die for this.

In London, Joe Slovo, who had escaped from South Africa just before the police discovered Lilliesleaf, led a march to protest against the trial. (Unable to return to his own country, Joe Slovo lived for twenty-seven years in the UK, Mozambique, Zambia, and Angola.) The United Nations also asked the South African government to stop the trial.

On 11 June 1964, the accused were found guilty, except for Lionel Bernstein, who was released. That night they prepared themselves for the death sentence. The next day, they entered the court for the last time. About 2,000 people waited outside the court. Mandela's mother had travelled all the way from Qunu, and sat with Winnie in the crowded court. Mandela and the other accused stood before the judge. Justice de Wet's face was serious, and he spoke slowly: 'The sentence in the case of all the accused will be one of life imprisonment.' The Rivonia trial was over.

The accused could hear the crowd singing *Nkosi Sikelel' iAfrika* as they were driven back to Pretoria prison. In the street, Winnie waited with their two daughters for a last sight of Mandela, but the crowd was too great. She drove

Winnie outside court with Zindzi and Zeni

home to Orlando and put the children to bed. Only then did she sit down and cry.

The prisoners were taken back to Pretoria Prison. Every night in the prison, African prisoners sang freedom songs. Before they slept someone always shouted 'Amandla!' and hundreds of voices answered 'Ngawethu!' That night was no different, but in the middle of the night Mandela, Sisulu, Mbeki, Mhlaba, Motsoaledi, Mlangeni, and Kathrada were woken and taken from the prison. They were flown in an old army plane to Robben Island to begin their sentence. Only black prisoners were taken to Robben Island, so the white prisoner Dennis Goldberg remained at Pretoria Prison.

6 Robben Island (1964–1970)

It was winter when the prisoners arrived on Robben Island, and the cold winter wind blew through their thin prison uniforms. The prison guards took them to a new building, specially built for political prisoners, separate from the ordinary African prisoners. There were about a thousand African prisoners on Robben Island, not all of them political.

On one side of the prison was a wall 6 metres high. Guards with guns and dogs walked along the top of the wall. All the guards were white, and all the prisoners were black.

The cells were about 2 metres square (when Mandela lay

Robben Island

down his head touched one wall and his feet touched the opposite wall). The walls were at least 60 centimetres thick, and always wet. The prisoners slept on the floor. They were given thin blankets, but in winter it was so cold that they kept their clothes on when they slept. Each cell had a small window, covered with metal bars, and double doors. During the day, the metal door was locked; during the night, the heavy wooden door was locked as well.

Each prisoner was given a prison number which was put on the door of the cell. Mandela was the 466th prisoner on Robben Island that year of 1964, so his number was 466/64 – a number that later became famous all over the world.

The guards woke the prisoners at 5.30 a.m. After cleaning their cells, the prisoners went outside for breakfast, which was porridge. The Indian and Coloured prisoners had sugar and bread as well, and it was not until 1979 that all prisoners received the same food. If the cells were untidy, the prisoners

Prisoners breaking stones

were punished. The prisoners then worked outside breaking stones without stopping until twelve o'clock, when one of the ordinary prisoners brought them some lunch.

Work continued until four o'clock, when the guards took the prisoners back inside. There they took a shower with cold sea water. This was the only time the prisoners were able to talk to each other.

At 4.30 p.m. the prisoners returned to their cells, where they ate supper alone (porridge again, with perhaps a vegetable as well). Each night at eight o'clock the night guard began walking up and down. He looked in at each prisoner through a small window. The one electric light in each cell was never turned off.

Later, the prisoners were able to study in the evenings until 10 or 11 p.m. The families of the prisoners had to pay for the books but many books were not allowed by the prison officials.

From the first day, Mandela protested about conditions on Robben Island, for example about the short trousers which the African prisoners had to wear. (Ahmed Kathrada was given long trousers because he was an Indian.)

A few weeks after their arrival on Robben Island, the guards brought two British newspaper men into the prison. They watched the prisoners as they worked and took a photograph of them. Then one of the prison guards called Mandela and a photograph was taken of Mandela and Sisulu. These were the only photographs of the prisoners during the long years on Robben Island.

Political prisoners could write and receive one letter (of 500 words) every six months. Sometimes the guards said, 'We have a letter for you, but we can't give it to you.' Often the prison officials cut out so much of the letters that the

Mandela and Sisulu in the prison yard, 1964

prisoners received only a few words. To wait for six months and then receive no letter was terrible. 'A letter was like the summer rain,' Mandela wrote. Just as the rain could make flowers grow in even the driest land, so a letter would bring him new hope.

Prisoners could also have one visitor every six months. The families of many of the prisoners lived far away and it was difficult and expensive for them to travel to Robben Island. Some men spent ten years or more on Robben Island without a single visitor.

For their first visit to Robben Island, a journey of about 1,600 kilometres, Winnie and Albertina Sisulu travelled together. Mandela talked to Winnie through a thick glass window, which had a few holes in it, while the guards stood behind them and listened. Their conversation had to be in English or Afrikaans; they were forbidden to speak Xhosa, and they were only allowed to talk about family matters.

Suddenly, the guard called, 'Time up! Time up!' Thirty minutes had passed, the visit was over, and Mandela walked back to his cell. It was two years before he saw Winnie again.

Other political prisoners arrived on Robben Island. Some of these were MK men, like Mac Maharaj who began his twelve years for sabotage in 1965. There were also members of other freedom groups, for example Zephania Mothopeng, a member of the PAC, and Eddie Daniels, a Coloured member of the Liberal Party. Eddie met Mandela for the first time when he began his fifteen-year sentence on Robben Island in 1964. He became one of Mandela's greatest friends in prison. 'Mandela is one of the greatest men in the world,' Eddie said afterwards. He explained that when he was ill on Robben Island, Mandela had taken care of him and cleaned his cell.

Between 1961 and 1991 (when the last political prisoners left the island) more than 3,000 African political prisoners were kept on Robben Island. The last ordinary African prisoners did not leave until 1996.

One morning the guards marched the political prisoners to the lime quarry which was cut into the side of a hill near the prison. The prisoners worked at the lime quarry for the next thirteen years. They had to break the rock in the quarry and then dig out the white stone and pack it on to trucks. Guards with guns watched the prisoners while other guards walked about and shouted at them. At twelve o'clock, the prisoners walked down the hill where they sat and ate their porridge. Lots of sea birds flew above them while they ate.

White dust covered the prisoners by the end of the day. Tears ran down their faces because the bright sunlight shone on the white lime and damaged their eyes. Again and again the prisoners asked for sunglasses, but three years passed before a doctor agreed that the prisoners needed sunglasses to protect their eyes.

On the way to the quarry, the prisoners passed a small white house, with a guard in front, where Robert Sobukwe (the leader of the PAC) was forced to live alone for six years. The prisoners were never able to see him or speak to him. He was alone for so long that in the end he forgot how to speak.

At first, the prisoners sang Xhosa freedom songs as they worked in the quarry, but the guards soon stopped them. However, in the quarry the prisoners were able to work in groups and they were able to talk together. Slowly, the prisoners organized a school for themselves while they worked, and Robben Island became known as 'the university'. For example, Walter Sisulu taught the history of the ANC and Kathrada taught the history of the Indian struggle.

In 1965, some officials from an international group visited Robben Island and Mandela was chosen by the other prisoners to meet them. Mandela protested about conditions on the island and asked for better clothes and food. He also asked for desks in the cells to help the prisoners to read and study better. In the end, the prison officials agreed to give the prisoners long trousers and desks (but no chairs). Mandela continued to ask for better conditions and later they were given chairs to sit on.

While in prison, Mandela became known by the name of his Thembu people, Madiba. Because of his dignity and his confident way of speaking, Mandela became the leader who continued to speak for the others, although he always discussed things with Sisulu. Fikile Bam, who was on Robben Island for ten years with Mandela, said later, 'He really did

1994 – revisiting the quarry on Robben Island

not fear people at all.' Even when Mandela was in prison uniform, he believed himself equal to anyone.

Mandela secretly gave advice as a lawyer to the ordinary prisoners in order to help them with their problems. Notes were passed to him, in boxes of matches, or hidden in food, and he wrote letters for them to prison officials and the courts. Mandela did not meet the men he was helping, but sometimes a prisoner who was bringing food whispered 'Thank you'. Prisoners who were leaving Robben Island hid messages from other prisoners in their clothes, and passed them on when they got home.

Political prisoners could never see newspapers, but sometimes they secretly took the guards' newspapers. Once Mandela was caught reading a newspaper in his cell and he was put in a small cell for three days, alone and without food. Prisoners were often put in a small cell without food, and only rice water to drink, as a punishment – for example, if they did not stand up when a guard came into their cell.

The ordinary prisoners heard more news about what was

Mandela's room in prison

happening in South Africa than the political prisoners did. They passed this news on to the political prisoners by hiding notes with the food. In this way, Mandela and his companions learned that Bram Fischer had gone 'underground'. For nearly a year Fischer avoided arrest, but in the end he was caught and found guilty of sabotage. He too was sentenced to life in prison and he joined the other white political prisoners in Pretoria Prison.

In September 1966, as the prisoners walked to their lunch at the lime quarry, the ordinary prisoner bringing the food whispered, 'Verwoerd is dead'. The Prime Minister had been killed in Parliament by someone who worked in the offices there. Conditions on Robben Island became more difficult because the guards were angry about the death of the Prime Minister. John Vorster was chosen as the new Prime Minister, and he continued Verwoerd's apartheid laws. When Vorster was asked about Mandela in 1975, he said: 'Anyone who wants to talk to me . . . [thinking that] Mandela is the leader of black South Africa can forget it.'

In spring 1968, Mandela's mother visited him on Robben Island. She travelled more than 1,000 kilometres all the way from Qunu, with Mandela's sister and Makgatho and Makaziwe, his second and third children with Evelyn. His children had grown into young adults, but his mother looked thin and old. A few weeks later, Mandela received the news that his mother had died. Mandela was not allowed to go to her burial, which added to his sadness. During the next few months, Mandela remembered the difficulties and suffering of his mother's life. He had put the struggle for freedom first, and because of that he had been unable to make her life easier.

In May 1969, the police woke Winnie at their home in Orlando, and took her out of the house as Zeni and Zindzi tried to hold on to her. Winnie (with twenty-one others) was charged with attempting to restart the ANC. She was questioned for five days and nights and then kept in prison, alone in a cell, for seventeen months. Finally, she was released without explanation. After hearing the news of her arrest, Mandela often lay awake at night, worrying about what was happening to Winnie and their daughters.

A few weeks later, one cold July morning, Mandela was called to the prison office and told that his eldest son, Thembekile (aged twenty-five) had been killed in a car accident. (Again, Mandela was not allowed to attend the burial.) Mandela returned to his cell and lay down. After the death of his mother, and the worry about his wife, this news filled him once more with terrible sadness. 'It left a hole in my heart that can never be filled,' he later wrote.

7 Prison and separation (1971–1984)

It was a hard and lonely life on Robben Island for the prisoners, so far away from their friends and families. Mandela said that prison was like a fire that tested a man: some became stronger, and others became less than they had been before. In the 1970s, sometimes the prisoners were taken to work at the beach. They pulled long, heavy plants from the sea on to the beach and left them to dry, and then they packed them onto the back of a truck. In the summer the sea was enjoyable, but in the winter the water was icy cold. However, the prisoners were glad to see the tall buildings of Cape Town across the sea, and they watched the clouds and sunshine moving across the flat Table Mountain which stood more than 1,000 metres high behind the city. The island was also home to groups of African penguins, and the prisoners enjoyed watching the fat black

The view of Cape Town from Robben Island

and white birds on the beach. The prisoners were also able to catch fish and cook them on the beach.

In 1975, Mandela's daughter, Zindzi, came with Winnie to visit him on Robben Island. The last time he had seen her, she was a little girl of three. Now she was a young woman of fifteen. She was shy towards the father she did not remember, but Mandela talked to her about the days when she was a baby. Nelson and Winnie decided to send their two daughters to school in Swaziland, where they could be safe from the police. Mandela worried about this, because he knew that the love of her daughters helped Winnie to survive.

That year, Mandela decided to write the story of his life. For four months, Mandela slept for only a few hours as he wrote for most of the night. Each day, Kathrada and Sisulu wrote notes on the pages he had written. Another prisoner, Laloo Chiba, copied the pages in his very small writing, putting ten pages on to one small piece of paper, and Mac Maharaj hid these small copied pages in the books he was studying. (When Maharaj was released from prison in 1976 he took these pages with him, and he kept them safe after he escaped from South Africa. Mandela used these pages when he wrote the full story of his life, *Long Walk to Freedom*, in 1994.) The prisoners secretly buried the 500 pages that Mandela had written, with the notes written on them by Sisulu and Kathrada, in three different places in the prison garden.

However, a few weeks later, when a wall was built in the garden, a packet of pages was discovered by the prison guards. The prison officials punished Mandela, Sisulu, and Kathrada: they were forbidden to study for four years.

The prisoners thought about escape all the time they were in prison, and in 1974 Maharaj and Mandela planned to escape when they were taken to see a doctor in Cape Town. But they were surrounded by guards with guns all the time, and they had to forget their plan. The prisoners always believed they were going to be free one day, and Mandela believed that more than anyone else. Fikile Bam said that Mandela believed that he was going to play an important part in bringing freedom to South Africa. While on Robben Island, Mandela learned to speak Afrikaans, and he talked to the guards in Afrikaans. He wanted to understand the Afrikaners, because he believed they were part of South Africa.

Township schoolchildren marching in Soweto

In the 1960s and 1970s, about 26 per cent of Africans did not have jobs. White miners were earning more than twenty times what African miners were earning. The 1970s were years of change in South Africa, though the prisoners did not immediately hear about these changes. In 1972, the Black Consciousness Movement was started by Steve Biko and other young black leaders. The Black Consciousness Movement was very popular with teachers and students. Its young leaders wanted to make black people proud of their own history and to help them to work together.

In 1976, 15,000 black schoolchildren marched through

Soweto to protest against a new law that teachers in African schools must use the Afrikaans language. Police began to shoot at the crowd, and several children were killed. During the next year, thousands of black children refused to go to school. More than 600 children were killed by police on the streets of the townships and thousands more were arrested.

Winnie Mandela was one of the black leaders who helped parents and families in the townships at this time. She was arrested in 1976, while her daughters were in Swaziland, and imprisoned in the Fort, Johannesburg, for five months. In May 1977, after she was released, twenty policemen arrived at her home in Orlando

West. Zindzi was at home with Winnie, and the police began to pack their furniture and clothes into a truck. They drove Winnie and Zindzi to an African township called Brandfort nearly 500 kilometres away. Winnie and Zindzi were left there in a small house without water or electricity, and Winnie was forbidden to leave Brandfort for seven years. People in the township spoke a language called Sesotho, which Winnie did not know, but while she was there, she started a school for young children and she helped to start a hospital for Africans.

In the 1960s and 1970s, the government forced more than 6 million Africans to move from their homes to the Bantustans, where there was not enough land for them to grow food. 'They came with guns and police . . . They brought us here, we do not know this place . . . What can we do now? We can do nothing.' These were the words of some of the people who were forced to move to the Bantustans. In the 1970s, white men in South Africa lived to the age of about sixty-five years. African men could expect to live to the age of about fifty years.

In September 1977, Steve Biko was arrested in Port Elizabeth and badly beaten by police. As he lay unconscious in the back of a truck, the police drove him more than 1,000 kilometres north to Pretoria Prison where he died. During the next few weeks, the police arrested every leader of the Black Consciousness Movement. Some of these prisoners were taken to Robben Island and for the first time Mandela contacted the new young African leaders. They sent secret notes to each other and some of these young men joined the ANC.

In 1977, work at the quarry ended. More guards were needed to control the younger prisoners, and Mandela and

Steve Biko

his group were now left in their own cells, where they could read, study, and write letters. Mandela also worked in the garden he had made. He grew tomatoes and vegetables, and gave some of them to the prison guards. Mandela had always enjoyed sport, and while in prison, he ran every morning in his cell for forty-five minutes. At this time one of the guards made a tennis court in the prison and Mandela began to play tennis with the other prisoners.

In 1978 Mandela's daughter Zeni married Prince Thumbumuzi Dlamini, the brother of King Mswati the Third of Swaziland. They had met while Zeni was at school in Swaziland. Later that year, Zeni visited her father, with her husband and baby daughter. It was the first time that the prison had allowed Zeni to visit her father since he went to prison fourteen years earlier. They were allowed to meet face to face, and Mandela was able to kiss his daughter and hold his granddaughter in his arms. 'I don't think a man was ever happier to hold a baby than I was that day,' he wrote afterwards. He chose the name Zaziwe for the baby, which means 'hope'. 'The name had a special meaning for me,' Mandela wrote, 'for during all my years in prison hope never left me – and now it never would.' He believed that this child would be part of a new South Africa, and that for her apartheid would be part of history.

In 1980, the prisoners were allowed to read some newspapers. However, the prison officials went through the papers first and cut out any stories they did not want the prisoners to see – including news of the 'Free Mandela' campaign. The ANC leader Oliver Tambo, who was still living outside South Africa, started this campaign. One South African newspaper had the story 'Free Mandela!' and pictures of Mandela were put up in London and other cities of the world. The South African government was becoming unpopular all over the world.

It was twenty years since the shooting at Sharpeville, and Zindzi Mandela spoke at a meeting of white students: 'I have not joined you as a daughter calling for the release of her father. I have joined as part of my generation who have never known what a normal life is.' The United Nations also called on the South African government to release Mandela and the other political prisoners.

One day in March 1982 Mandela was told to pack his things: he was leaving the island. With no time to say goodbye to their companions of eighteen years, Mandela, Walter Sisulu, Raymond Mhlaba, and Andrew Mlangeni were put on the boat to Cape Town. They had no idea where they were going. Mandela looked back at the island, as the sun went down. It was not a place that he liked, but it was a place that he knew. He wondered if he would ever see it again. The prisoners were taken from the boat and driven to Pollsmoor Prison, a few kilometres outside Cape Town, where Ahmed Kathrada joined them a few months later.

Pollsmoor Prison was a modern prison, and Mandela and the others were the only political prisoners there. They were given a large room to share on the third floor, with real beds, a separate bathroom, and a large open place on the roof where they could walk during the day. Mandela soon started a garden here and he worked in it every day. He grew

vegetables which he gave to the prison kitchen and to some of the guards.

Although conditions in Pollsmoor were more comfortable than on Robben Island, and they were given better food, it was a world without trees. The men missed their own cells, and they missed their other companions and the sea and the birds of Robben Island.

In May 1984, when Winnie visited him in Pollsmoor, the guard took her into a visiting room where Mandela was waiting. There was no glass wall between them. For the first time for twenty-one years, Mandela was able to kiss his wife and put his arms around her.

8   Walking to freedom (1985–1994)

Mandela and the other men had been in prison for more than twenty years, and many of their friends were now dead. Bram Fischer became very ill while he was in prison; he was released in 1975, and died soon afterwards. Robert Sobukwe died in 1978 at the early age of 54. Griffiths Mxenge, a lawyer who was part of the Free Mandela Campaign, was murdered in 1981. In 1982, Ruth First (the wife of Joe Slovo) was killed by a bomb in Maputo, Mozambique, where she was living. Joe Gqabi, who had been in prison on Robben Island for many years with Mandela, was also murdered in 1981.

There was more and more violence in South Africa. MK's sabotage of railway lines and apartheid offices also increased.

'Free Mandela' campaign, London

The government tried to introduce a new separate parliament for the Indian and Coloured people but more than 80 per cent of Indian and Coloured voters refused to vote in this election.

World opinion against apartheid was growing. In 1984, Archbishop Desmond Tutu, the famous South African church leader, was given the Nobel Peace Prize. Archbishop Tutu was born in Transvaal in 1931, the son of a teacher. In 1975 he began to speak out against apartheid when he became the first African leader of the South African Council of Churches. He called for equal rights for everyone, and for non-violent protests by black South Africans. He wanted other countries to stop buying anything from South Africa, to force the government to change.

In America, Jesse Jackson and other black leaders spoke against the apartheid system. Edward Kennedy, John F. Kennedy's brother, visited South Africa and went to meet Winnie Mandela in Brandfort (though he was not allowed to visit Mandela himself). But Minister of Justice Kobie Coetsee allowed Lord Bethell (a member of the European Parliament) and Professor Dash (a well-known American lawyer) to visit Mandela in prison, in order to prove to the world that Mandela was in good health. Mandela told both these visitors that he wanted a free and equal country, where all adults were able to vote for the government. He explained that if the government changed, the ANC would stop the use of violence. After he returned to Europe, Lord Bethell asked the governments of Europe to persuade the South African government to free Mandela.

In January 1985, President P. W. Botha stood up in Parliament and offered Mandela his freedom if he stopped using violence. Mandela heard this on the radio and he

Archbishop
Desmond Tutu

immediately replied. When Winnie visited him, he gave her the words he had written, and his daughter Zindzi read her father's words to a crowd in Soweto's stadium. For the first time for more than twenty years, the people of South Africa heard the words of Mandela.

'I am a member of the African National Congress,' he began. 'I have always been a member of the African National Congress and I will remain a member of the African National Congress until the day I die.' He asked President Botha to give up violence by putting an end to apartheid. And he would not take this 'freedom' that was offered to him. How could he be free when the people's organization – the ANC – was banned? How could he be free if he – or anyone else – had to carry a pass? He refused to make any promises. His final words to the people were, 'Your freedom and mine cannot be separated. I will return.'

Later that year, while Mandela was ill in hospital, Kobie Coetsee (1931–2000), who seemed to be a new kind of Afrikaner leader, came to visit him. From the beginning Coetsee saw him as a future president. Although Mandela was a prisoner, and wearing hospital clothes, he was a natural leader and full of dignity. From that time, Coetsee wanted everyone to know that he was valuable.

But when Mandela returned to Pollsmoor Prison, he was put by himself in a different part of the prison. Mandela protested to the prison officials that his new cell was dark and cold. If Mandela wanted to see the other political prisoners, he had to ask for a meeting, and they met in the visitors' room, where the guards listened to their conversations.

Early in 1986, a group of important world leaders, led by General Obasanjo of Nigeria and Malcolm Fraser of Australia, arrived in South Africa to report to their governments on the situation in the country. For the first time since 1964, Mandela wore a suit, instead of his prison uniform. Kobie Coetsee joined the meeting between Mandela and the group, and Mandela told him that the time had come to negotiate. However, the day before the group were going to meet Mandela for the second time, President Botha ordered bombs to be dropped on ANC soldiers in Botswana, Zambia, and Zimbabwe. The group left South Africa immediately, but Mandela began to have secret talks with Kobie Coetsee.

The violence in South Africa continued to get worse. By the 1980s, South Africa had the highest number of people punished by death of any country in the world. Crowded houses in the towns and in the Bantustans caused many Africans to die from serious illness. For example, in the 1980s, 75 per cent of people ill with TB (a serious illness brought to South Africa more than 100 years ago from Europe) were Africans, and only 1 per cent were white. In the 1980s, there was one doctor for every 300 white people. For Africans, the situation was very different: there was one doctor for 90,000 people.

In July 1988, Mandela's seventieth birthday was remembered around the world with more calls for his freedom. But it was a difficult time for Mandela. He learned that his home in

Orlando West had been burned down. Many old photographs and other valuable, personal things were lost. Mandela also had a problem with his chest, and he often felt ill. At last, a doctor came to see him and said he was seriously ill. He was taken to hospital where doctors said that, probably because of his cold cell, he was suffering from TB.

After some weeks in hospital, Mandela began to get better. In December 1988, he was moved to live in a prison guard's house in Victor Verster Prison near Cape Town. On his first day in the house, Kobie Coetsee visited him and brought him some bottles of wine as a present. Coetsee told him that this would be his last home before he became a free man. Later, speaking of his release from prison, Nelson Mandela said that he was helped when preparing for his release by the story of Pandit Nehru, who wrote about what happens when you leave prison. In Victor Verster, Mandela was allowed to live a more normal life. He was visited by members of the ANC and other freedom groups, as well as by members of his family. In 1989, on his seventy-first birthday, he had a birthday party and his wife, children, and grandchildren were all allowed to come. It was the first time in his life that he had been able to have his whole family with him.

In 1989, F. W. de Klerk became President of South Africa. Nobody knew much about de Klerk, who was Minister of Education and had been in political life since 1972, but he soon showed everyone that he wanted to change the situation in South Africa. In October, he told parliament that the Pollsmoor political prisoners, and several other Robben Island prisoners, were going to be released. Walter Sisulu, Raymond Mhlaba, Ahmed Kathrada, and Andrew Mlangeni were brought from Pollsmoor to say goodbye to Mandela. They all knew that Mandela would soon be released too.

The men were taken to Johannesburg, and then released. A crowd of 80,000 people in Soweto welcomed the prisoners back home. The crowd sang the banned ANC song, *Nkosi Sikelel' iAfrika*.

In February 1990, President de Klerk told parliament that the bans on the ANC, the PAC, and the Communist Party were going to be lifted and the political prisoners released. At last the time to negotiate had arrived. On 10 February, Mandela was taken to meet President de Klerk who told him that he was going to be released the next day. Mandela telephoned Winnie and Walter Sisulu in Johannesburg, and they immediately flew to Cape Town. Mandela was only able to sleep for a few hours that night.

On 11 February 1990, as the world watched on their televisions, Mandela walked with dignity towards the gate of Victor Verster Prison. He was tall, handsome, and looked younger than his seventy-one years. He smiled at the waiting crowd as he walked to freedom. 'As I finally walked through

Mandela leaving Victor Verster prison

those gates to enter a car on the other side,' he wrote later, 'I felt – even at the age of seventy-one – that my life was beginning anew'. His prison days were over.

Mandela was driven, with Winnie, to City Hall in Cape Town. The crowd was so great that at first they could not get out of the car. As he stood in front of the crowd, he lifted his hand and said: *'Amandla! Amandla!'* He told the crowd that apartheid had no future in South Africa, and that talks between the government and the ANC were beginning: 'I therefore place the remaining years of my life in your hands,' he told the people.

Mandela spent his first night of freedom at Archbishop Tutu's home in Cape Town, and then the next day he flew to Johannesburg. Thousands of people surrounded his old home in Orlando West so they flew by helicopter to Soweto Stadium. There 120,000 people were waiting to welcome Mandela back to Soweto. He told the crowd that his return to Soweto filled his heart with happiness, but he also felt a deep sadness, because their suffering under apartheid was not over. But apartheid would end soon, and the violence in the townships must also end.

That night, Mandela returned to Number 8115 Orlando

Mandela with Winnie and Sisulu
at the Soweto football stadium

Oliver Tambo returns to South Africa

West. People sang and danced outside the house, full of happiness that he was home again. The four-roomed house had been rebuilt after the fire, and at last Mandela knew that his prison days were over.

Soon after he was released, Mandela flew to Lusaka, in Zambia, to talk to the leaders of the ANC, and then he travelled to other countries in Africa. He went on to Stockholm to visit Oliver Tambo who was seriously ill. (Tambo returned to South Africa soon afterwards; he died in 1993.)

Back in South Africa, Mandela was involved in talks with the leader of the Zulu people, Chief Buthelezi, about the violence between Inkatha, the Zulu people's group, and ANC members. But in spite of their talks, the violence continued. Mandela travelled through the country and was told by the people that the police were involved in the violence. Mandela met with President de Klerk and asked him to do more to stop the violence. The ANC leaders continued to negotiate with the government about how to organize the new South Africa.

The political difficulties Mandela faced were matched by personal difficulties. Winnie Mandela, after many years of suffering in Brandfort, had returned to Johannesburg in 1984. She became the leader of a group of young men, called the Mandela United Football Club, which became more and more involved in violence. In 1989 several of these young men were involved in the murder of a fourteen-year-old boy, Stompie

Seipei. The ANC leaders tried to stop Winnie's involvement with the violence, but she refused to listen to them.

After he was released from prison, Mandela discovered that his wife had fallen in love with a young lawyer. In April 1992, with Walter Sisulu and Oliver Tambo by his side, Mandela told the world that he was separating from his wife. His love for Winnie and her love for him had helped him to survive the long years in prison. He did not blame his wife, and he had loved her inside and outside prison from the moment he first met her. He asked people to understand the pain that he had gone through. Mandela knew that the struggle for freedom had taken him away from his family.

At the end of 1993, Nelson Mandela and President de Klerk were given the Nobel Peace Prize for their work for peace in South Africa. Mandela spoke about his dream of a new South Africa. Then he went on to speak about de Klerk. The President, he said, accepted the truth that terrible suffering had been caused by apartheid, and accepted that the government needed to negotiate. Later, de Klerk said that although Mandela had made mistakes, most South Africans believed in him as a leader because he understood the fears and hopes of the nation.

The journey towards freedom was not easy, and the violence continued, but on 27 April 1994, the first election for all people in South Africa took place. Among those who voted for the first time in their lives was the ninety-year-old wife of the Nobel Peace Prize winner, Chief Luthuli (who had died in 1967). The violence stopped, and some people queued for eight hours in order to vote. One woman said, 'I've been waiting forty-six years. I don't mind waiting a little longer.' It took several days for the votes to be counted. The ANC received nearly 63 per cent of the votes, winning

252 of the 400 seats in the national parliament. 'Free at last! This is a time to heal the old wounds and build a new South Africa,' Mandela said.

On 10 May, a hot autumn day in Pretoria, Mandela became President of South Africa, with his daughter Zeni by his side. He promised to obey the laws of the new South Africa and to give himself to the people of South Africa. About 60 world leaders were there, including Nyerere from Tanzania and Kaunda from Zambia. Boutros Boutros-Ghali from the United Nations was there, and Hillary Clinton and Jesse Jackson were there from the United States. A crowd of 60,000 people sang the two national songs: *Nkosi Sikelel' iAfrika* and *Die Stem*, the Afrikaans song of the years of apartheid. More than 300 years of white government ended. The long struggle for freedom was over.

President Mandela with de Klerk and Mbeki

9 The new South Africa (1994–1999)

Mandela had made his walk to freedom, but there were other journeys ahead of him. 'We have not taken the final step of our journey,' he wrote, 'but the first step on a longer and even more difficult road.' As President of South Africa Mandela had many journeys, often difficult ones, to make.

The new government showed Mandela's view of a new South Africa, where all groups of the nation had a part to play – black and white South Africans, Indians, Coloured, communists, and other political groups. It was a new kind of government, which no other nation in the world had tried. Kathrada and Mlangeni, Mandela's old friends from Robben Island, were elected to the new parliament. Among the new ministers were Chief Buthelezi, Minister of Home Affairs, and Joe Slovo, Minister of Housing. Mac Maharaj, a prisoner for many years on Robben Island with Mandela, became Minister of Transport. Abdullah Omar, one of the lawyers who had visited the political prisoners on Robben Island, became Minister of Justice. Fikile Bam became Judge-President of the Land Claims Court in 1995.

The members of Mandela's government had an extremely difficult job ahead of them: to change the system of government without driving businesses out of the country. People of all nations wanted Mandela to come and visit them, and he travelled to many countries to meet governments and businesses. He used his visits to talk to businesses and ask them to work with the new government in South Africa. In 1995, for example, he travelled to India, Japan, Russia, China, France, New Zealand, and the United States.

Mandela also worked for peace in Africa, and travelled to Tanzania, Lesotho, Botswana, Uganda, Libya, and Mozambique. Jessie Duarte, Mandela's secretary while he was President, travelled with him, and noticed that he was always surprised that people knew him. Sometimes she was frightened by the large crowds surrounding him. 'It was also difficult,' she said, 'because he could never take a private walk anywhere.' Mandela solved this problem by getting up early in the morning and taking a long walk at 5 a.m.

As the new government got to work, South Africa began to experience less violence. Mandela wanted to recognise the history of the different peoples of South Africa, and to lead them to a peaceful life together. It was not long before Mandela was loved by many South Africans, because of his dignity and the love he showed to all people. Most of the time, Mandela refused to wear suits. Instead, he preferred to wear bright shirts, which became known in South Africa as Madiba shirts. 'I want to be comfortable,' he said. 'I want to dress like a man who is living in Africa, because that's where I live.'

In 1990 South Africa needed about 1.3 million new homes, but in the year 1992 only 50,000 homes were built. The new government arranged money for houses for the poorest people, but this only happened slowly. The ANC government planned to build 1 million new houses in five years, to bring clean water no more than 200 metres from each home, and to bring electricity to all schools and hospitals within two years. During 1994, the government brought electricity to 250,000 homes.

By 1995, more than 7,000 MK members had joined the South African army. The government also gave all South Africans the right to own land and planned to return land to those who had lost it because of the apartheid laws.

The government wanted the people of South Africa to be able to talk to each other about their suffering under the apartheid system. In 1995 Archbishop Desmond Tutu was chosen by Mandela to look into the crimes of apartheid. For two years Archbishop Tutu and the Truth and Reconciliation Commission heard more than 20,000 people talk about torture by the police and about the terrible things that had happened during the years of apartheid. For example, police officers told the commission how they beat Steve Biko before his death in 1977.

Mandela and Tutu

Apartheid officials told the commission that Botha had agreed to the bomb which exploded at the central office of the South African churches in 1988. F. W. de Klerk was one of the few political leaders who came forward to talk about what happened while he was president. He appeared before the commission in August 1996, and he apologised for the pain and suffering caused by the National Party. But he refused to answer questions about the bombs used against black groups in the 1980s.

Nelson Mandela started his Children's Fund in 1995 after he met children on the streets of Cape Town. He remembers: 'We were driving back to the president's house in Cape Town one cold winter's evening, when I saw a group of street children and stopped to talk to them. They asked me why I love them.' Mandela was surprised by this question, but the children said that they knew he loved them because every time he got money from abroad he used some of it to help them. Mandela organized the Children's Fund to help children of South Africa, and he promised to give one third of his own money to the Fund. He began to ask everyone for money for the Fund, and he used his visits abroad to organize the Children's Fund in London, New York, and Toronto. Between 1996 and 1998, 36 million rand (then worth about 6.5 million US dollars) was collected to help thousands of children.

Mandela's love of sport continued while he was President. During most of the years of apartheid, South African teams were unable to play against other nations. But since 1994, sport has shown that it is strong enough to mend old wounds. When the Springboks (the South African rugby team) won the Rugby World Cup in Johannesburg in 1995, Nelson Mandela put on the number six shirt of the team's captain

Mandela at the Rugby World Cup, 1995

– Francois Pienaar, a white Afrikaner – and the two shook hands as Mandela gave Pienaar the Cup. Later, Mandela said that this was one of the happiest moments of his life, when South Africa won something as a nation. Mandela said to the captain of the team, 'Thank you very much for what you have done for South Africa.' And Pienaar replied, 'Thank you for what you have done.' In one generous moment, four hundred years of suffering and bitterness suddenly seemed to disappear.

Football is the most popular sport in South Africa, and in 1992 the first international game for thirty years was played in South Africa. The national football team Bafana Bafana – 'the Boys' – won the African Cup of Nations in 1996 in Johannesburg. Mandela was in the crowd of 90,000 who watched the final game and came on to the field when the team lifted the Cup. In 1998 Bafana Bafana played in the World Cup finals for the first time. And for four weeks in 2010, South Africa will be the centre of the world, as teams from all over the world play for football's World Cup.

In 1997, Mandela began to give more and more political responsibility to Thabo Mbeki. Mbeki was the son of Govan Mbeki, who was imprisoned with Mandela on Robben Island. Thabo Mbeki joined the ANC when he was fourteen years old and he escaped from South Africa in 1962, at the age of nineteen. He went to university in Britain, and worked for the ANC in Britain, the Soviet Union, and Zambia. He returned to South Africa in 1990 and joined the ANC leaders who were negotiating with the apartheid government. Now, as Deputy President, Mbeki was the second most important political leader after Mandela.

The years of loneliness after Mandela separated from Winnie ended in 1998 when he married Graça Machel on his eightieth birthday. Graça Machel was married to Samora Machel, the President of Mozambique, until his death in a plane crash in 1986. President Machel had helped the ANC for many years and Mandela secretly sent a message from prison to Graça Machel after President Machel's death. He met her for the first time in 1990 when he visited Mozambique.

In February 1999, Mandela spoke for the last time in parliament. He listed the ways his government was helping to change the lives of many. Water had reached 1.3 million South Africans and electricity had reached 58 per cent of the population. 'We can and shall build the country of our dreams!' he said.

In June 1999 there were elections again in South Africa. The ANC received 66 per cent of the votes and Thabo Mbeki

Mandela and
Graça Machel,
1998

was elected president. Leaders from 130 countries watched as Mandela's government ended and the new President Mbeki promised to obey the laws of South Africa. Mandela and Mbeki lifted their hands as the crowd watched. This was the beginning of a new government, Mbeki said, but it was also a day of thanks to those who pulled the country out of apartheid.

It was time for Mandela to step away from national life and to enjoy time with his children and grandchildren. He moved to Qunu, Transkei, where he had built a home similar to the prison guard's house where he lived in Victor Verster Prison.

The new President gave a dinner to say thank you and goodbye to Mandela as he began this new life. Mandela said that it would not be easy to rest while millions were still poor, but it would make him happy to know that people were joining together to continue the work of the past. 'Though I shall not be seen as often as before,' he said, 'I shall be among you and with you as we enter the African century; working together to make a reality of our hopes for a better world.'

10

A quieter life (2000–2013)

South Africa has become popular with tourists from all nations of the world, and in 2005 more than one and a half million tourists visited the country. The most popular place for tourists is still Table Mountain in Cape Town. Over a thousand metres high, Table Mountain is home to beautiful plants and animals and has views over the beaches and sea, with Robben Island not far away. Many tourists visit Robben Island, to see the cell where Mandela spent so many years, and the lime quarry where the prisoners worked. Tourists can also visit his old home in Soweto, Number 8115 Orlando West.

Johannesburg has grown, and Rivonia is now part of the city. Large houses have been built on the fields near Lilliesleaf Farm. When he was released in 1990, Mandela searched the quiet streets before he found the house where he lived as a driver called David Motsamayi. The farm is now being developed as a museum and centre for visitors. It will be a

Mandela's new home in Qunu

place to remember the leaders who lived in Lilliesleaf and show how important they were. The centre will help visitors to understand what the struggle was about.

Many tourists visit the wild coast of Mandela's childhood, with its green hills and beautiful beaches, and make the journey to Qunu, the small village where he lived as a child and where he still lives for many months of each year.

South Africans are proud of their country, and Africans have become richer since 1994. Many have built their own businesses and taken jobs in government, and are hungry for more success. The government has built nearly 2 million houses and by 2005, most homes had electricity, nearly half of homes had telephones, and South African television companies were making their own programmes. But there were thousands of Africans who still did not have jobs or land, and who were still very poor.

Nelson Mandela's part in the history of South Africa did not end when he stepped away from national life. He continued to learn from the suffering of his people and from his own personal suffering. HIV/Aids has become the greatest problem in South Africa; in 2004 over 6 million South Africans were living with HIV. In 2002, Mandela began to work to help those with HIV/Aids. He asked his Children's Fund to build houses for children who had lost their parents through Aids, and the Fund now helps 150,000 of these children.

In 2003, Mandela began to organize a new music campaign

The 46664 concert in Cape Town, 2003

for people with HIV/Aids. He used his old prison number, 46664, for this campaign. There was a large concert in Cape Town, where Mandela spoke to the crowd. The singers Angelique Kidjo, Baaba Maal (from West Africa), Beyoncé (from the United States), Bob Geldof, Bono (from Ireland), Ms Dynamite (from the UK), Ladysmith Black Mambazo, Yvonne Chaka Chaka (from South Africa), and many others were involved in the concert. Since then, there have been concerts in Spain and Norway. The money from the campaign is used for programmes to care for people with HIV/Aids.

The campaign also asks both famous and ordinary people to help those with Aids. For example, many people help the Ikageng Itireleng Aids Ministry (begun by Carol Dyantyi), in Orlando, Soweto. This centre cares for more than 300 children who have lost both their parents to Aids. Mandela has friends in all nations, and many of them (for example, Bill Clinton and Will Smith, from the United States, and the footballers Ronaldo and Luis Figo) are helping his work.

Mandela has experienced the death of many of his friends and family. In May 2003, Walter Sisulu died and Mandela spoke at his burial of the pain that he felt when he saw his friends go. 'From the moment when we first met, Walter has been my friend, my brother,' he said. And he ended with a call to the people: 'The spear of the nation has fallen . . . Let us pick up the spear, now to build a country after the example that Walter Sisulu has set for us.'

In April 2004, Mandela was invited to parliament to speak about the ten years of South Africa's freedom. He remembered the excitement and happiness of those first days of freedom. He asked people not to forget the terrible past from which they came, but to let it remind them of how far they had come and how much they had done. His wish, he said, was that South Africans should never stop believing in goodness. South Africa had become an example to many, and it showed that good could grow among those who were prepared to work with others and to believe in the goodness of people. As Mandela left parliament, everyone sang, 'Rolihlahla Mandela, freedom is in your hand, show us the way to freedom in Africa.'

A few weeks later, Mandela decided to spend more time with his family and friends. He wanted a much quieter life, and rest from all his work. On Mandela's birthday in 2004, all his family came to visit him, and at the party both Winnie and Graça helped him to cut the birthday cake.

But the sadness in his life was not over. In January 2005 Mandela told the world that his son, Makgatho, a lawyer like his father, had died of Aids at the age of fifty-four.

Mandela and Graça at Makgatho's funeral

Makgatho's young children were left without parents, since their mother had died of Aids in 2003. Mandela, who had spent months visiting his son in hospital, said that it was important for people to talk about Aids. 'The only way to make it appear like a normal illness, like TB, like cancer, is always to come out and say somebody has died because of HIV/Aids.' (In 2004, Chief Buthelezi also said that his son had died of the illness.)

President Mbeki and Archbishop Desmond Tutu joined thousands of people in Qunu for Makgatho's burial. Nothing could hide the pain in Mandela's face as he sat with his wife, daughters and grandchildren during the burial, and stood with a yellow rose in his hand as his son was buried.

And yet Mandela could not rest completely, and he still accepted some invitations. In February 2005, Mandela visited London for the Make Poverty History campaign. Bob Geldof introduced Mandela to the crowd in Trafalgar Square, and called him 'the president of the world!' Mandela's smile was on his face again as he spoke to the

Nelson Mandela in Trafalgar Square, London, 2005

crowd of 22,000 people. 'I say to all those leaders, do not look the other way, do not hesitate. Recognize that the world is hungry for action, not words.'

A few months later, in June 2005, at the age of nearly 87, Mandela travelled to Tromsø, in Norway, for the 46664 concert. 'This has indeed been a long journey from Johannesburg in South Africa to Tromsø in Norway. But we are pleased to be here. Tonight, the people of Tromsø can stand tall and proud,' he said. He thanked the people of Tromsø for their work. Then he said, 'You have become part of us and so you are now all Africans.'

On 5 December 2013, Nelson Mandela died at the age of 95. For more than sixty years, the name of Nelson Mandela was heard first in South Africa and then across the world. Mandela spent nearly thirty years in prison, but those years did not destroy him. Instead, they made him strong and patient and gave him experience in negotiating and working with other people and in listening to their problems. Mandela was one of the world's greatest leaders.

GLOSSARY

area part of a town or country

ban *(v & n)* to say that something is not allowed; to stop somebody from doing something

campaign a plan to do a number of things in order to get a special result

cell a small room for one or more prisoners in a prison

charge to accuse somebody of a crime so that there can be a trial in court

committee a group of people chosen to decide things or do a special job

communist a person who believes in communism, a system of government in which everyone is equal

concert a public performance of music

court the place where a judge decides if a person has done something wrong

desire *(n)* something that you want very strongly

dignity calm and serious behaviour that makes other people respect you

elect to choose somebody to be a leader by voting for them; *(n)* **election**

equal having the same rights as other people

forbid to say that somebody must not do something

force *(v)* to make somebody do something that they do not want to do

freedom not being a slave; being able to do or say what you want

fund money that will be used for something special

generation all the people who were born at about the same time

government a group of people who control a country

guilty having done something that is against the law

history things that happened in the past

including having something as part of a group

injustice something that is wrong and unfair

member somebody who belongs to a group or organization

mine *(n)* a deep hole or tunnel in the ground where minerals like gold are dug

minister someone who is in charge of a government department

negotiate to discuss something in order to reach an agreement

official a person who does important work for a large organization

organization a group of people who work together for a special purpose

parliament the group of people elected to decide the laws of a country

political connected with questions of government

porridge a thick wet food made by cooking cereal with water

power (1) electricity; (2) the ability to do things

protest (*v & n*) to speak or act against something you disagree with

province a large area of a country that has its own local government

quarry a place where stone is dug from the ground

release to let a person go free

right ability by law to have the chance to do something, e.g. to vote, go to school etc

sabotage (*n*) damage that you do to something as a way of protesting

sentence (*n & v*) punishment for a crime given by a judge in a court

share to have something at the same time as somebody else

struggle to try very hard to do something when it is difficult

suffering a feeling of pain or sadness

surround to be all around something

system a group of ideas or ways of doing something

torture (*n & v*) to cause great pain to somebody in order to make them give information or to punish them

treason the crime of doing something that could cause danger to your country

truck a large vehicle for carrying heavy loads

United Nations an organization of many countries that tries to solve world problems peacefully

violence behaving in a way that can hurt or kill people or damage things

vote to choose somebody in an election

wealth a large amount of money etc that a country owns

Nelson Mandela

ACTIVITIES

ACTIVITIES

Before Reading

1 **Read the back cover of the book, and the introduction on the first page. Are these sentences true (T) or false (F)?**

1 South Africa has always been a poor country.
2 Nelson Mandela spent a long time in prison.
3 Life for black South Africans was good in the 1950s.
4 Nelson Mandela became president of South Africa.

2 **Which of these words do you think you will find in the book? Why?**

island, uniform, e-mail, the Netherlands, oil, football, election, horse racing, tourists, spear, desert, schoolchildren

3 **Four of these sentences about Nelson Mandela are correct. Which ones do you think they are?**

Nelson Mandela . . .
1 . . . ran away from home when he was a young man.
2 . . . never married.
3 . . . studied law at university.
4 . . . worked in a gold mine for a short time.
5 . . . once tried to kill the president of South Africa.
6 . . . wrote a book while he was in prison.

ACTIVITIES

While Reading

Read Chapters 1 and 2, then complete the sentences with the correct names.

Chief Jongintaba / Justice / Dr Daniel Malan / Evelyn Mase / Miss Mdingane / Walter Sisulu / Oliver Tambo

1 Mandela's first teacher, _____, gave him the name 'Nelson'.
2 After Mandela's father died he lived with his uncle, _____.
3 Mandela met _____ when they were students at Fort Hare.
4 Mandela ran away to Johannesburg with his cousin _____.
5 _____ helped Mandela to find a job in Johannesburg.
6 Mandela fell in love with a student nurse called _____.
7 _____ wanted black and white people to live separately.

Read Chapter 3, then circle the correct words.

1 The government forced black people out of their homes in *Sophiatown / Kliptown*.
2 For two years, Mandela was forbidden to leave *Johannesburg / Orlando West*.
3 The *Defiance / Freedom* Charter said that everyone should be able to vote for the government.
4 Winnie was Mandela's *second / third* wife.
5 The police killed sixty-nine people at a protest in *Sharpeville / Cape Town*.
6 At the end of the treason trial, Mandela was found *guilty / not guilty*.
7 Prime Minister Verwoerd said that black Africans should be called *Nkosi / Bantus*.

**Before you read Chapter 4, can you guess what happens?
Choose Y (yes) or N (no) for each sentence.**

While Mandela is 'underground' . . .
1 . . . he is shot by a policeman. Y / N
2 . . . he secretly leaves South Africa. Y / N
3 . . . he kills somebody. Y / N
4 . . . he is arrested and put in prison. Y / N

**Read Chapter 4. Choose one of these question-words for
each question, and then answer the questions.**

How / How long / What / Where / Who / Why
1 . . . did Mandela have to leave Wolfie's flat?
2 . . . was Mandela's name when he worked for MK?
3 . . . received the Nobel Peace Prize in 1961?
4 . . . did MK members plan their work?
5 . . . did Mandela and his wife dress at the trial in Pretoria?
6 . . . was Mandela on Robben Island before he was taken
     back to Pretoria?

Read Chapter 5, then fill in the gaps with these words.

accused / lawyer / protest / sabotage / sentence / torture / weapons
1 In the 1960s the police began using _____ while
   questioning prisoners.
2 Bram Fischer was a _____ at the Rivonia trial.
3 Mandela was charged with _____.
4 The court could give the death _____ for sabotage.
5 The police had found hundreds of papers but no _____ at
   Lilliesleaf Farm.
6 Bruno Mtolo spoke against the _____ at the Rivonia trial.
7 In London, Joe Slovo led a march to _____ against the
   trial.

Read Chapter 6, then match these halves of sentences.

1 From the first day, Mandela protested . . .
2 In winter it was so cold . . .
3 The electric light in each cell . . .
4 The prisoners were able to study, . . .
5 Prisoners could have one visitor . . .
6 Mandela talked to Winnie through a window while . . .
7 At first, the prisoners sang Xhosa freedom songs, . . .

a) that the prisoners slept in their clothes.
b) the guards stood behind them and listened.
c) every six months.
d) was never turned off.
e) about conditions on Robben Island.
f) but the guards soon stopped them.
g) but their families had to pay for the books.

Read Chapter 7, then answer these questions.

1 Why was Zindzi shy when she visited Mandela in prison?
2 What did Mandela write while he was in prison?
3 Which language did Mandela learn while he was in prison?
4 Where did Steve Biko die?
5 Who started the 'Free Mandela' campaign?

Before you read Chapter 8, can you guess what happens? Choose Y (yes), N (no), or M (maybe) for each sentence.

Mandela . . .
1 . . . becomes seriously ill. Y / N / M
2 . . . is sent back to Robben Island. Y / N / M
3 . . . is released from prison. Y / N / M
4 . . . separates from his wife. Y / N / M

Read Chapter 8, then circle *a*, *b*, or *c*.

1 _____ offered Mandela his freedom if he stopped using
violence.
a) P. W. Botha   b) Kobie Coetsee   c) Jesse Jackson
2 In Victor Verster Prison, Mandela lived in a _____.
a) small cell   b) guard's house   c) shared room
3 A book by _____ helped Mandela to prepare for release.
a) Desmond Tutu   b) Walter Sisulu   c) Pandit Nehru
4 The 'Mandela United Football Club' was led by _____.
a) Nelson   b) Zindzi   c) Winnie
5 In 1993, the Nobel Peace Prize went to Mandela and _____.
a) F. W. de Klerk   b) Desmond Tutu   c) P. W. Botha
6 In the 1994 election, the ANC received _____ of the votes.
a) 33 per cent   b) 63 per cent   c) 93 per cent

**Read Chapter 9. Are these sentences true (T) or false (F)?
Rewrite the false ones with the correct information.**

1 Mandela chose only black Africans for his government.
2 Most of the time, Mandela liked to wear suits.
3 Mandela collected a lot of money to help poor children.
4 The South African football team won the World Cup in 1995.
5 Mandela married again when he was eighty years old.
6 When Mandela left the government, he moved to Pretoria.

**Before you read Chapter 10, can you guess what happens?
Circle Y (yes) or N (no) for each sentence.**

Mandela . . .
1 . . . stops travelling to other countries. Y / N
2 . . . marries again. Y / N
3 . . . tries to become president again. Y / N
4 . . . experiences more sadness in his life. Y / N

ACTIVITIES

After Reading

1 Use the clues to complete the puzzle.

1 Thick food made with cereal and water, often given to prisoners.
2 A place where stone is dug from the ground.
3 A political system that separated black and white people.
4 A long, difficult fight for justice.
5 A language spoken in South Africa by people whose families came from the Netherlands.
6 Being able to say or do what you want.
7 When a country chooses its leaders.
8 Large black and white birds that live by the sea.
9 Damage done to important property (like power stations or railway lines) on purpose.

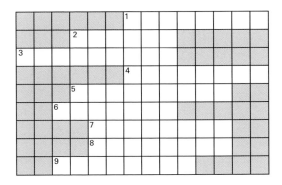

What is the tenth word, hidden in the puzzle? Write the names of four people in the book who have had this position in South Africa.

2 **Kathrada, who has just left prison, is talking to a reporter. Put their conversation in the right order and write in the speakers' names. The reporter speaks first (number 11).**

1 _____ 'Well, as an Indian I was given warmer clothes and better food, for example, than the Africans like Nelson.'

2 _____ 'Very soon, I hope. I saw him at Victor Verster recently, and he's in good spirits. We're old friends.'

3 _____ 'And how were you punished?'

4 _____ 'That's true, but Nelson hasn't been released yet.'

5 _____ 'They were terrible for me. But they were even worse for Nelson.'

6 _____ 'You were both on Robben Island, weren't you?'

7 _____ 'At first, yes – but later the guards discovered that Nelson was secretly writing his life story, with my help.'

8 _____ 'In what way?'

9 _____ 'That's right. We were taken there after the Rivonia trial.'

10_____ 'But you were both allowed to study, weren't you?'

11_____ 'So, Ahmed Kathrada, now you are a free man!'

12_____ 'And when do you think that will happen?'

13_____ 'We were forbidden to study for four years. It was a difficult time. But now we must think about the future!'

14_____ 'What were conditions like there?'

3 **How has South Africa changed? Write sentences comparing South Africa now and in the 1970s. Use some of these words to help you.**

tourists, Bantustans, pass, vote, equal, torture, Robben Island, Aids

4 **Perhaps this is what some of the people in the book are thinking. Who are they, and what are they thinking about?**

1 'Johannesburg, the city of gold! When we're there, my father won't be able to tell us who to marry. My cousin and I will have fun! But how will we get the money for our tickets?'

2 'I never see him. And our children are always asking where he is. I know his work is important, but I'm not interested in politics. I'm leaving! I'm going to my brother's house.'

3 'Why is that car in front driving so slowly? Oh, no – there are two more cars right behind me, and they're all full of white men. It's the police. If I run away, they'll kill me!'

4 'I'm nervous! There are thousands of people in this stadium. But my father's message is important. He's not going to agree to anything just for his freedom. He wants his country to be free. I must make sure everyone hears.'

5 **Do you agree or disagree with these sentences? Why?**

1 People should never use violence against the government.
2 Equality is impossible, because some people are more talented than others.
3 Conditions in prisons should be reasonably comfortable.
4 Courts should have the power to give death sentences for serious crimes.

6 **Find out more about one of the events, places, or people mentioned in the book, and make a poster. For example:**

Steve Biko, The Sharpeville Massacre, Robben Island, Soweto, Table Mountain ,Chief Luthuli

Websites like www.wikipedia.org and www.southafrica.com will give you more information.

ABOUT THE AUTHOR

Rowena Akinyemi is British, and after many years in Africa, she now lives and works in Cambridge, though she still goes to Africa every year on holiday. She has worked in English Language Teaching for twenty-five years, in Africa and Britain, and has been writing ELT fiction for fifteen years. She has written several other stories for the Oxford Bookworms Library, including *Rainforests* (Factfiles) and *Love or Money?* (Crime and Mystery). She has also adapted several stories for the same series, and her adaptation of *Cry Freedom* (True Stories) was a finalist in the Language Learner Literature Award, an international award for graded readers, in 2004.

She has four children and is a keen football fan, supporting Manchester United. She enjoys country holidays in Britain – a long walk over hills or along cliffs in Wales, followed by a cream tea in a village teashop. But she also enjoys days in London shopping, walking on Hampstead Heath, looking at historical buildings, going to a concert or the theatre. She likes all sorts of music, especially African music, jazz, classical music, and Bob Dylan, and enjoys reading crime fiction and biographies.

As a student Rowena went on marches in London against apartheid, and she returned to the subject of South Africa when she worked on *Cry Freedom*, which is set in the apartheid years of the 1970s. She has never met Nelson Mandela, but while she lived in Nigeria she met Chief Buthelezi, who was also an important political leader in South Africa and had a position in Nelson Mandela's first government. She also met Archbishop Desmond Tutu and his wife in London in 1994.

OXFORD BOOKWORMS LIBRARY

Classics • Crime & Mystery • Factfiles • Fantasy & Horror
Human Interest • Playscripts • Thriller & Adventure
True Stories • World Stories

The OXFORD BOOKWORMS LIBRARY provides enjoyable reading in English, with a wide range of classic and modern fiction, non-fiction, and plays. It includes original and adapted texts in seven carefully graded language stages, which take learners from beginner to advanced level. An overview is given on the next pages.

All Stage 1 titles are available as audio recordings, as well as over eighty other titles from Starter to Stage 6. All Starters and many titles at Stages 1 to 4 are specially recommended for younger learners. Every Bookworm is illustrated, and Starters and Factfiles have full-colour illustrations.

The OXFORD BOOKWORMS LIBRARY also offers extensive support. Each book contains an introduction to the story, notes about the author, a glossary, and activities. Additional resources include tests and worksheets, and answers for these and for the activities in the books. There is advice on running a class library, using audio recordings, and the many ways of using Oxford Bookworms in reading programmes. Resource materials are available on the website <www.oup.com/elt/gradedreaders>.

The *Oxford Bookworms Collection* is a series for advanced learners. It consists of volumes of short stories by well-known authors, both classic and modern. Texts are not abridged or adapted in any way, but carefully selected to be accessible to the advanced student.

You can find details and a full list of titles in the *Oxford Bookworms Library Catalogue* and *Oxford English Language Teaching Catalogues*, and on the website <www.oup.com/elt/gradedreaders>.

THE OXFORD BOOKWORMS LIBRARY
GRADING AND SAMPLE EXTRACTS

STARTER • 250 HEADWORDS

present simple – present continuous – imperative –
can/cannot, must – *going to* (future) – simple gerunds …

Her phone is ringing – but where is it?

Sally gets out of bed and looks in her bag. No phone. She looks under the bed. No phone. Then she looks behind the door. There is her phone. Sally picks up her phone and answers it. *Sally's Phone*

STAGE 1 • 400 HEADWORDS

… past simple – coordination with *and*, *but*, *or* –
subordination with *before*, *after*, *when*, *because*, *so* …

I knew him in Persia. He was a famous builder and I worked with him there. For a time I was his friend, but not for long. When he came to Paris, I came after him – I wanted to watch him. He was a very clever, very dangerous man. *The Phantom of the Opera*

STAGE 2 • 700 HEADWORDS

… present perfect – *will* (future) – *(don't) have to, must not, could* –
comparison of adjectives – simple *if* clauses – past continuous –
tag questions – *ask/tell* + infinitive …

While I was writing these words in my diary, I decided what to do. I must try to escape. I shall try to get down the wall outside. The window is high above the ground, but I have to try. I shall take some of the gold with me – if I escape, perhaps it will be helpful later. *Dracula*

STAGE 3 • 1000 HEADWORDS

… should, may – present perfect continuous – *used to* – past perfect –
causative – relative clauses – indirect statements …

Of course, it was most important that no one should see
Colin, Mary, or Dickon entering the secret garden. So Colin
gave orders to the gardeners that they must all keep away
from that part of the garden in future. *The Secret Garden*

STAGE 4 • 1400 HEADWORDS

… past perfect continuous – passive (simple forms) –
would conditional clauses – indirect questions –
relatives with *where/when* – gerunds after prepositions/phrases …

I was glad. Now Hyde could not show his face to the world
again. If he did, every honest man in London would be
proud to report him to the police. *Dr Jekyll and Mr Hyde*

STAGE 5 • 1800 HEADWORDS

… future continuous – future perfect –
passive (modals, continuous forms) –
would have conditional clauses – modals + perfect infinitive …

If he had spoken Estella's name, I would have hit him. I was so
angry with him, and so depressed about my future, that I could
not eat the breakfast. Instead I went straight to the old house.
Great Expectations

STAGE 6 • 2500 HEADWORDS

… passive (infinitives, gerunds) – advanced modal meanings –
clauses of concession, condition

When I stepped up to the piano, I was confident. It was as if I
knew that the prodigy side of me really did exist. And when I
started to play, I was so caught up in how lovely I looked that
I didn't worry how I would sound. *The Joy Luck Club*

BOOKWORMS · FACTFILES · STAGE 4
Great Crimes
JOHN ESCOTT

It is more than forty years since the Great Train Robbery. But what happened to the rest of the money that was taken? Two million pounds has never been found. Perhaps some of the robbers would like to know the answer to this question too . . .

Many great crimes end in a question. Who really killed President Kennedy? What happened to Shergar? Who knows the truth about Azaria Chamberlain? Not all the answers are known. Join the world's detectives and discover the love, death, hate, money and mystery held in the stories of the great crimes.

BOOKWORMS · FACTFILES · STAGE 4
The History of the English Language
BRIGIT VINEY

About a quarter of the people in the world today speak or use English. In homes and schools, offices and meeting rooms, ships and airports, people are speaking English everywhere.

How has this happened? How did English begin, and what will become of it in future? The history of the English language is a journey through space and time, from thousands of years ago to today and beyond, and to all parts of the world. Come on that journey and meet the monks and soldiers, the kings and scientists, the printers, poets, and travellers who have helped to make the English of today.